What's the Matter with Henry?
The True Tale of a Three-Legged Cat

What's the Matter with Henry?
The True Tale of a Three-Legged Cat

Cathy Conheim and BJ Gallagher

Design by Bob Walker

ASPCA Humane Issues Award 2006
Best Gift Book 2006 Cat Writers' Association

Written by Cathy Conheim and BJ Gallagher
Photography by Cathy Conheim
Design by Bob Walker (bob@catshouse.com)
Photo illustration by Bob Walker
Additional photography by Tim Brittain (twbrit@cox.net)
and Bob Walker
Henry cookie by Francois Goedhuys (www.funcookies.com)

What's the Matter with Henry?
The True Tale of a Three-Legged Cat

ISBN 0-9679576-4-8
Softcover: First Edition, September 2007
Printed in Korea (sales@onlineprintings.com)

Breakthrough Press
P. O. Box 135
La Jolla, California 92038

Henry's books available at:
www.henrysworld.org
www.breakthroughpress.com

Henry jm™

For kritters and kids everywhere
who long to be loved just as they are.

Cathy and Donna were best friends.
They had known each other for a long time
and had many things in common —
including a dislike of cats.

Cathy especially —
for her mother had taught her to hate cats.
Cats kill birds,
and Cathy's mom loved birds.

Donna didn't really hate cats —
she just didn't like them very much.

Cathy and Donna did love dogs.

They had a gorgeous black poodle
named Dolly,
and they loved her very much.
Dollydog was big and beautiful and smart,
with a strong spirit
and a lively personality.

Cathy, Donna, and Dollydog were happy together
in their home in the mountains.

Life was good.

Then one afternoon a stranger crept into their house …
an odd stranger,
a stranger with no name except Kitty.
A little tiny thing
weighing no more than a few pounds,
he scooted in through the front door
which someone had left ajar.

He was a small brown tabby kitten,
with stripes all over,
and special stripes making an M
on his forehead.

A fearless spirit,
Kitty walked right up
to a startled Dollydog
and touched his nose
to hers.

"What's this?"
Cathy wondered
as she watched their odd meeting.
"Where did that cat come from,
and what's he doing
going nose-to-nose with Dolly?"

Then, as if that weren't enough,
Kitty's three sisters
(Kitty, Kitty, and Kitty)
also scampered in
through the open door.

"Uh-oh," Cathy thought,
"this is not a good thing."

She went to get Donna.

Together they picked up
the four kittens,
one in each hand,
and put them back outdoors,
making sure the door was closed
this time.

"Cats!" Cathy exclaimed.
"In our house!
Can you believe it?"

Donna watched the kittens
through the window.
They played by the door for a while,
and then wandered off among the trees.

"They don't seem to belong to anyone,"
she said to Cathy.

The days went by,
and Cathy and Donna
would sometimes see the kittens
around the trees …
playing hide and seek in the leaves,
taking turns
pouncing on one another.

Donna enjoyed watching their antics.
Occasionally Cathy would watch too.

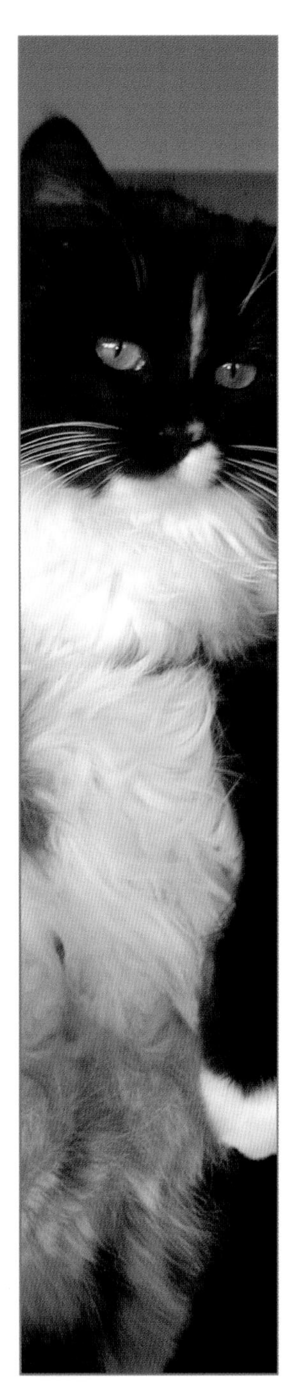

One day Cathy noticed
that the four kitties outside
were no longer four —
now there were only three.

"I wonder what happened to the other one,"
she said to Donna.

"I don't know," Donna replied.
"Maybe we should go look for him."

So look they did —
high and low,
far and wide,
in every nook and cranny —
until finally they found him
curled up inside
Dolly's doghouse.

Cathy reached in
and scooped him up.

"Something's wrong with him,"
she said to Donna.
"One of his front paws
is hanging funny.
I'm not sure,
but I think it might be broken."

"Oh my,"
Donna replied.
"We'd better take him
to a veterinarian
right away."

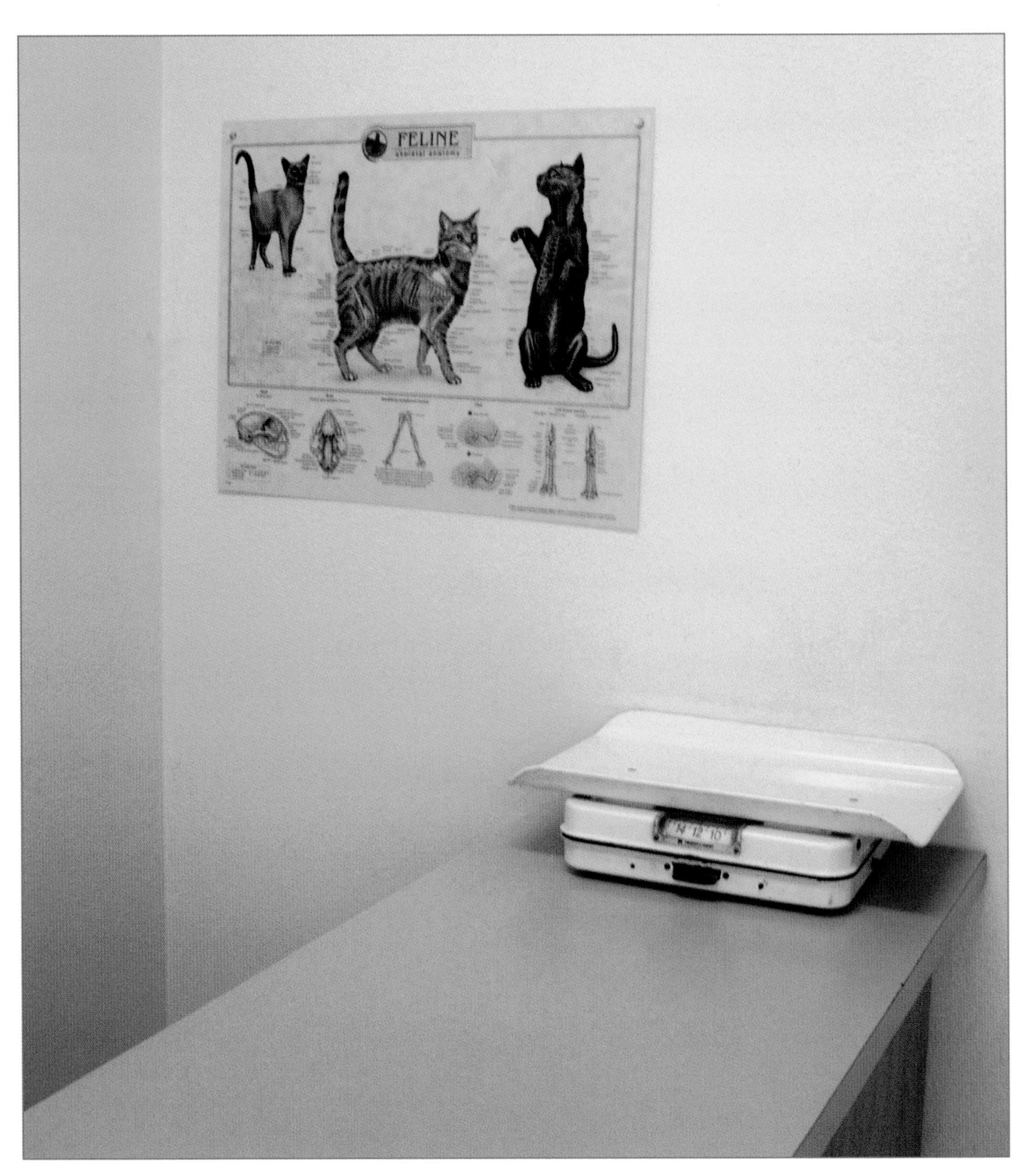
FELINE

So off to the nearby animal hospital they went.
The good doctor there
checked the kitten's limp leg.

"I'm sorry," the doctor said,
turning to Cathy and Donna,
"he's hurt his front leg very badly,
and it can't be fixed."

"Oh my," Donna whispered.

"There are only three choices,"
the doctor continued.
"If you do nothing about his leg,
soon it will get infected,
and the kitten will get sick and die.
It would be much kinder
to give him a shot
that will make him die quickly
with no pain.
I can do that,
or I can operate and remove his leg,
which will save his life."

ANIMAL HOSPITAL

Cathy and Donna looked at each other.
They were stunned
by what the doctor had said.

They didn't know what to do,
so Cathy took the kitten in her arms
and they went outside to talk it over.

"Well, there's no way we can have a cat,"
Cathy told Donna.

"Yes, you're right,"
Donna replied.
"We don't even like cats.
If we let Nature take its course,
he'll die a slow death.
That would be cruel.
I think we have no choice
but to help him die quickly
and peacefully.
You take the kitten back inside
and tell the doctor, OK?"

"Ohhh … OK," Cathy said slowly.

She looked down at the kitten
in her lap.
He looked back at her
with complete trust.

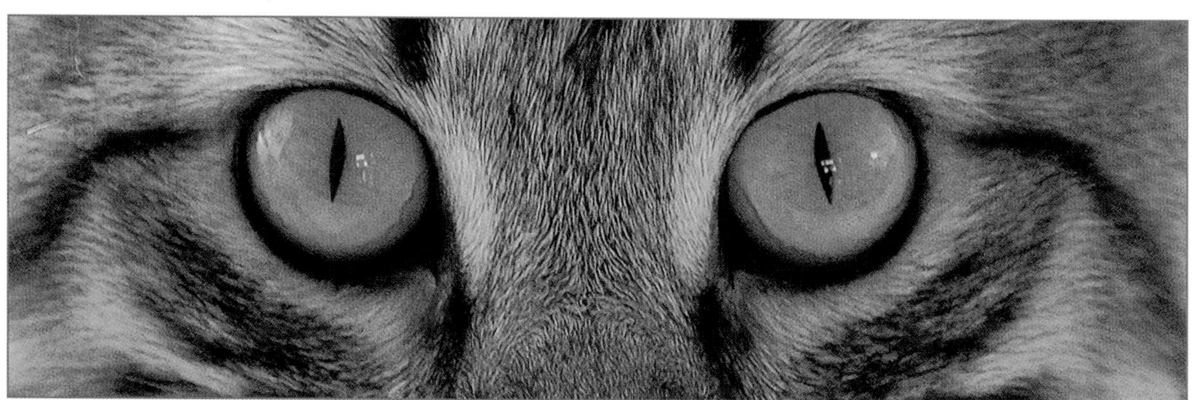

"I think maybe *you* should tell the doctor,"
Cathy said,
and handed the kitten to Donna.

"OK," Donna sighed.
She looked at the kitten
with his little hurt leg.

He began purring softly
as he met her gaze
with his wide gold-green eyes.

Donna and Cathy looked at the kitten.

The kitten looked back at them.

Nobody moved.

Donna's eyes filled with tears.
"Oh Cathy, we can't let him die,"
she said.

Now Cathy's eyes teared up, too.
"I can't bear it!"
she cried.

"OK, then," said Donna.
"Let's tell the doctor
to save the kitty's life,
even if he can't save the leg.
Then we'll see
if we can find the little guy
a good home."

"Who will want a three-legged cat?"
asked Cathy.

"I don't know
who will take him,"
said Donna.
"But we can't let him die.
We just can't."

So it was settled.

The doctor did the operation
and removed the kitten's leg
to save his life.

The kitten was young
and strong
and healthy,
so he came through the surgery just fine.

When he went to sleep at the animal hospital
he had four legs,
and when he woke up
he had only three.

He was very brave
through the whole thing.

When the kitten was well enough
to leave the animal hospital,
Cathy and Donna took him to their house
to care for him.

They stocked up on cat supplies
because they knew that
he would need their help
and some time to heal.

Cathy and Donna would also use this time
to find him a good home.

"What shall we call him?"
Cathy asked Donna.
"We can't just call him 'Kitty.'"

"You're right," said Donna.
"He should have a proper name —
something for a boy."

They played around with many names
and finally settled on Henry —
a fine name for a boy cat.

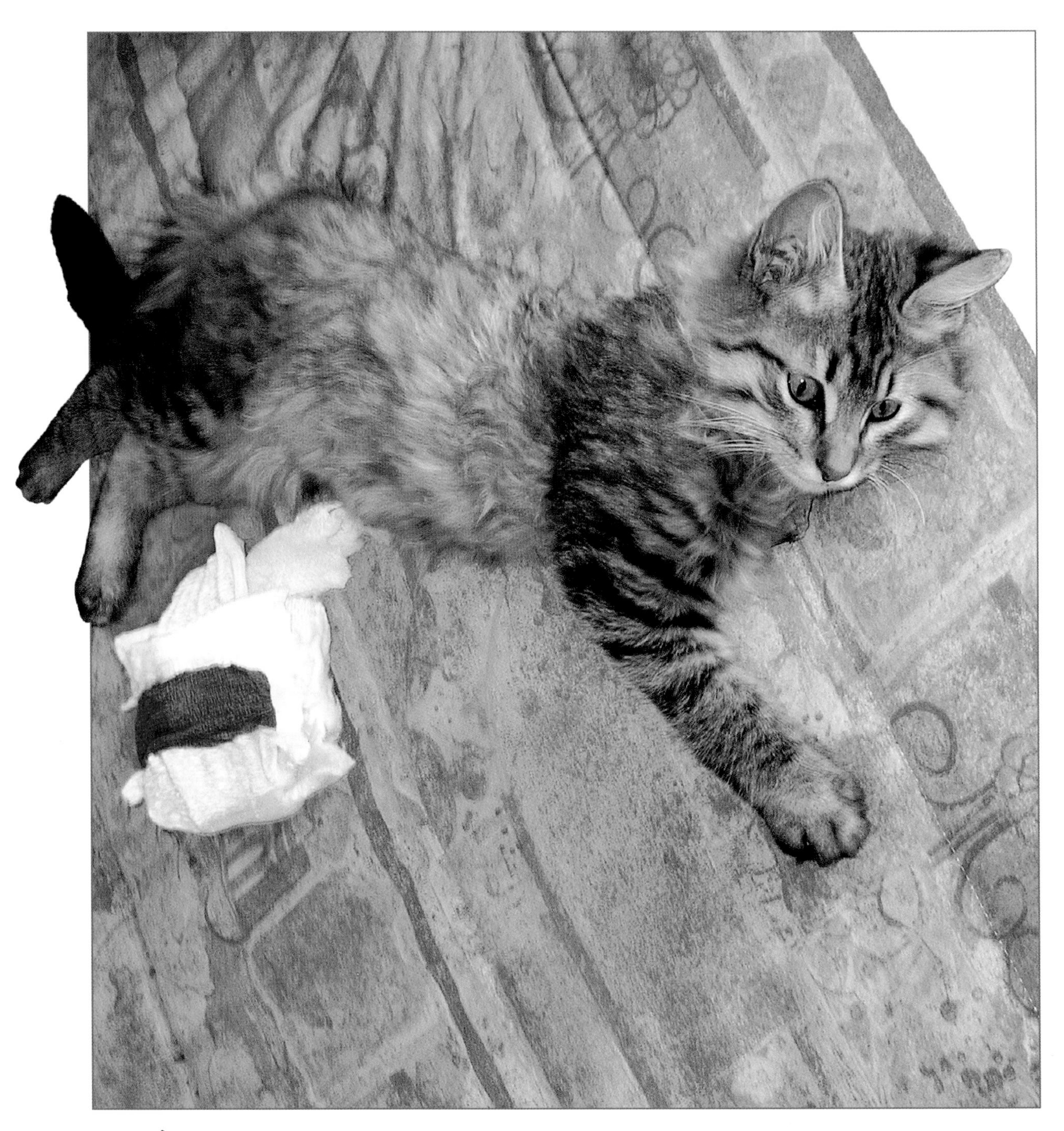

Donna checked the kitten's bandages.

"I wonder what happened to Henry …
Cathy said as she watched.
"How did his leg get hurt so badly?"

Had he fallen out of a tree?
Had he gotten hit by a car?
Had he been attacked by a forest animal?

They asked Henry, and he tried to tell them,
but all he could say was, "Meow."

Cathy and Donna looked at Henry,
then looked at each other.
They didn't understand "Meow."

Whatever had happened to Henry
was something only Henry would know.

Dollydog didn't know what to make
of this new creature in her house.

Was this a toy for her to play with?
Was this a snack for her to eat?

This little striped kitten with only three legs
hopped up to Dolly
and tried to make friends.

Cathy and Donna watched nervously.
"What will Dolly do?"
they wondered.

Would Dolly bark?
Would she growl?
Would she be too rough with Henry?

"What a brave little guy,"
Cathy thought.

Dolly sniffed at Henry
and watched him a lot,
but she didn't try to hurt him.

Time passed,
and Henry was healing well.

"It's time to find Henry a home,"
Cathy said.
"This house is no place for a cat."

"You're probably right,"
Donna agreed.
"But you have to admit,
he's *so* cute.
Look at the way
he tries to snuggle up to Dolly
when he wants to sleep."

Cathy thought he was cute, too,
but she didn't say so out loud.

"Henry probably misses his sisters,"
Cathy pointed out.
"I'm sure he must have slept
all cuddled with them at night."

"Yes, but he can't live outside
with them anymore,"
Donna replied.
"The doctor said
he has to be an indoor kitty ."

"Well, if he has to stay indoors,
then I'll make him a pen,"
Cathy said.
"I don't want him wandering
all over the house.
He might get into things he shouldn't."

Cathy made a circular space
with a folding fence
she bought at the pet store.
In it she put a bed,
a litter box,
his food and water,
some toys,
and a tall, wonderful cat scratching post.

After everything was in place,
she plopped Henry down
into his new living quarters.

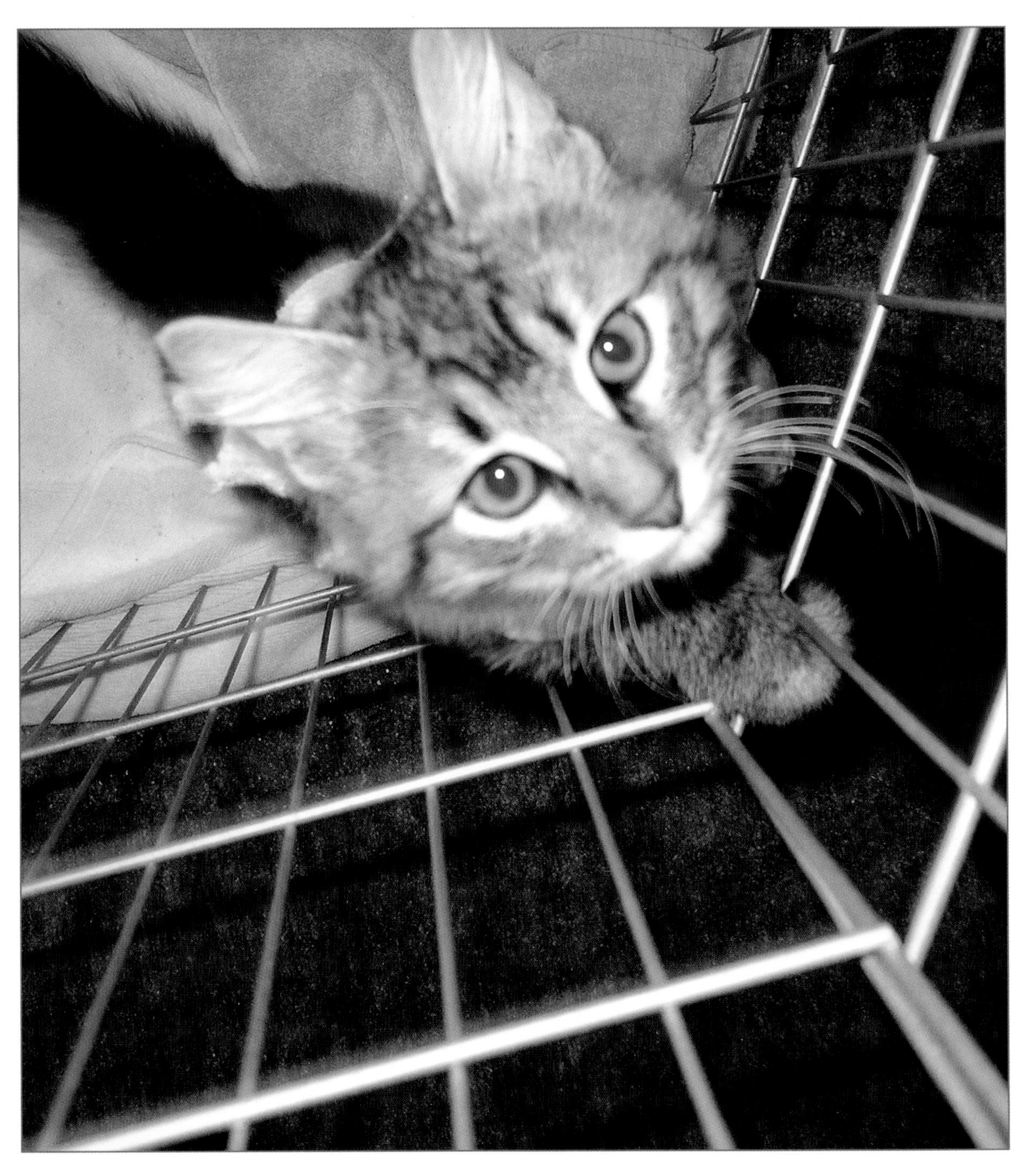

Henry took one quick look
at the walls around him
and decided he wanted none of it.

A pen might be fine for a dog
but it's no place for a cat —
so with one big jump,
Henry leapt right out!

"Hmph!"
harrumphed Cathy.
"I didn't know
a three-legged cat
could jump so high,"
she said.
"I'll have to put a top
on the pen,
to keep him inside."

So she got a large sheet —
big enough to cover the entire thing —
and she fastened it in place
with some clothespins.

"Now it's not just a pen —
it looks like a fort of some kind,
or a circus tent,"
Donna remarked.

"Yes, well, whatever it takes
to keep him in one place,"
Cathy muttered.
She didn't want Henry
to have the run of the house,
especially at night
while she was sleeping.

She put him back
inside his fort,
turned off the lights,
and went to bed.

Cathy still had a lot to learn about cats —
and especially about Henry.

She had no idea
who she was dealing with.

For Henry was determined
to have his way with her house —
as well as her heart.

Night after night,
Henry would find a way
out of his tent,
and then explore for hours
in the dark.
His night vision was good
and his paws were silent.
He was quiet and careful
as he could be.
But once in a while
he would make a little noise
and startle Cathy awake.

"That cat!"
Cathy would grumble in the dark.
"What's he into *now*?!"

Then she'd get up
and go searching for him.

"You scamp!"
she'd scold him
as she put him back
in his tent,
adding more clothespins
to keep the sheet in place.
"What's the *matter* with you, Henry?"
Cathy growled,
all grumpy and tired.
"Don't you know
that nights are for sleeping?"

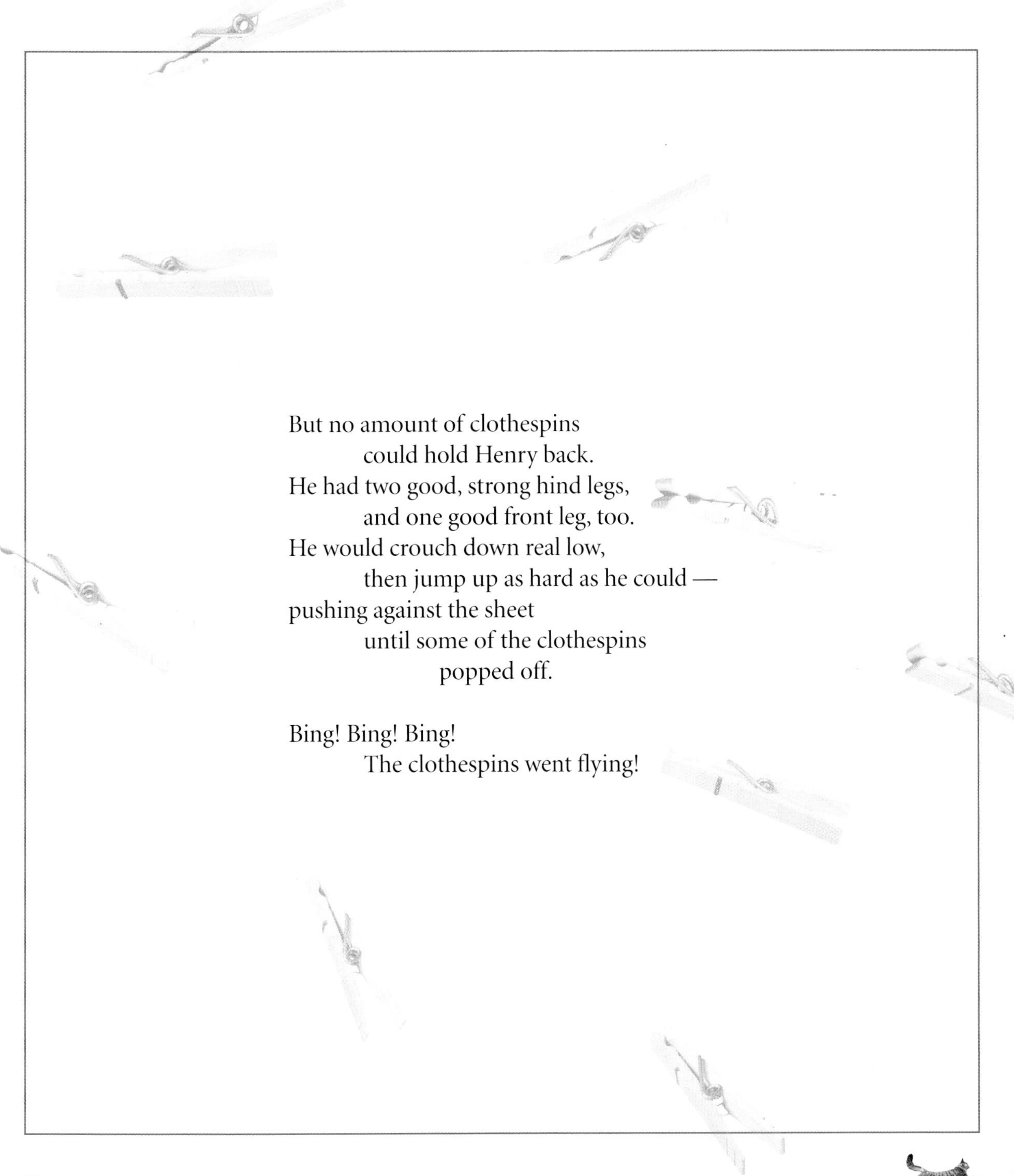

But no amount of clothespins
could hold Henry back.
He had two good, strong hind legs,
and one good front leg, too.
He would crouch down real low,
then jump up as hard as he could —
pushing against the sheet
until some of the clothespins
popped off.

Bing! Bing! Bing!
The clothespins went flying!

Then Henry climbed out of the pen,
as easily as if he had four legs
instead of just three.

For Henry was smart and strong.
He knew what he wanted
and was determined to get it.
He didn't let the lack of a leg
hold him back one bit!

Henry had the body of a kitten —
but the heart of a *lion.*

As weeks went by
this contest of wills continued …

Cathy continued her efforts
to keep Henry under control.

But his longing for freedom
could not be squashed —
not by pens,
sheets,
clothespins,
tents,
or any other kind of cage
that Cathy could build.

Henry was determined
not to be limited by walls —
neither the walls of his pen
nor the walls in anyone's mind about cats.

Cathy finally realized
she had met her match in Henry.

She came to understand
that a cat needs to be a cat.

Henry had insisted on being himself …
not a dog in a pen,
not an animal that sleeps at night,
not a critter to be confined in a tent.

And Cathy learned to accept Henry,
just as he was.

"Hmmmm,"
Cathy thought out loud,
"just himself, that's who he is …
'just me' …
jm …
That's what I'll call him
from now on,"
she said,
"Henry jm!"

And Henry jm became his new name.

"It's a funny thing,"
Cathy said to Donna one day,
as they were watching
Henry play with Dolly.
"I've spent my whole life hating cats
without knowing anything about them."

"Yes, you're right,"
Donna replied,
"it's easy to reject something
or someone
you don't know."

"Well, now that I know Henry,
I don't think I dislike cats anymore,"
Cathy said,
reaching down to pet him.
"And I certainly don't dislike *this* one."

Cathy looked at Donna,
and Donna looked back at her.
They could tell they were thinking
the same thing at the same time.

"I think Henry came into our lives for a reason,
Cathy said softly.
"He gave up a leg
and his outdoor life
to show us something about ourselves."

"I think you're right,"
Donna replied.
"Henry has shown us
that we don't get to decide
what happens to us in life —
but we *do* get to decide
how we respond to it.

"If we have courage and
we're willing to keep trying,
then, just like Henry,
we can overcome
problems of all kinds."

Cathy nodded,
smiling at Donna.

"I don't think we need to look
for a home for Henry anymore,"
she said quietly.

"Really?" Donna asked.

"Yes, really," Cathy replied.

"Home is where you're loved.
I think Henry *is* home."

THE END . . . ?

no, it's just the beginning.

Kibble for Thought

Henry prepared these pages for anyone who would like to explore life's lessons a little more.

Hate Is Learned

It is easy to hate what we do not know. Hate does not let us get acquainted with potential friends. When we come to know someone, human or animal, it is hard to hold onto hate.

Hard Things Happen

It is not what happens to us that makes us who we are, it is how we respond to those events and what we choose to do about our feelings. We all choose our responses.

Be True to Who You Are

Be proud. Do not let others make you into anything you are not. Know when to listen and how to listen to your inner voice. Be Just You!

Play the Hand You Are Dealt

No "ifs," "ands," or "buts"; no "if onlys"; and no blame. Play the hand life gives you to the best of your ability, no matter what challenges come your way.

Connect with What You Care About

You cannot do everything, but you can do something that makes a difference to somebody, and you can connect with others who care about the same things you do.

Henry's Homework for Humans

Is there a story about something in your life that you could tell Henry?

If you wanted Henry's help with something, what would it be? Who else in your life could help you with this?

Sometimes Henry feels that dog lovers do not understand cats and that he must help people to understand them. Who in your life does not understand you? What help can you give them so that they understand you better?

Henry likes to find a quiet place to spend some time each day. Where is your quiet place, and why is it special to you?

Sometimes Henry wants to hide. Are there times when you want to hide, and why?

Lots of people said Henry could not do some things when he became a three-legged cat. Do people tell you that you cannot do some things? How do you prove them wrong?

What does being a good friend mean to you? What can you do to show people that you are a good friend?

Is there anything about you that makes you feel like Henry? What is it?

What do you think other people should know about Henry?

What are the most important lessons you have learned from an animal in your life, or from a special friend?

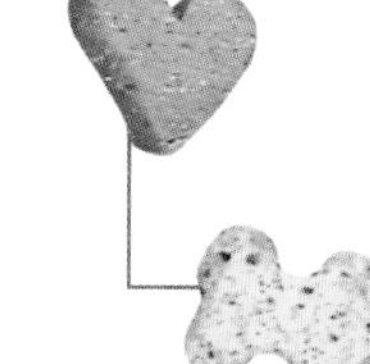
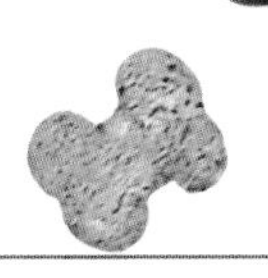

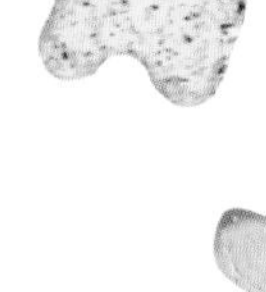

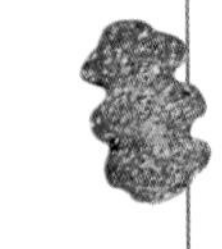

Henry's Mission

Henry's story doesn't end with him winning the hearts of his human companions. His life was saved for a reason, and Henry is now a cat with a mission. He has dedicated himself to raising funds so that other animals who are hurt, sick, or homeless can have a chance to heal, get well, and find good homes with loving humans.

All proceeds from the sale of this book are being donated to cat and dog rescue groups, shelters, zoos, and other animal welfare causes.

If you or your group would like to use this book (or Henry's first book, *Henry's World*) for fund raising to benefit an animal cause, please contact Henry c/o Breakthrough Press, P.O. Box 135, La Jolla, California, 92038 or henry@breakthroughpress.org.

Henry thanks you for your support of his four-footed (and three-footed) furry friends, as well as critters with feathers, fins, or scales. Your contributions are truly appreciated by those who can't speak for themselves.

Treat yourself to
www.henrysworld.org

Books and Goodies available to help Henry help others.

Coming Soon!
Henry's original
Pawedcast